SPORTS
ALL-ST★RS

DAK
PRESCOTT

Jon M. Fishman

Lerner Publications ◆ Minneapolis

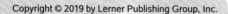

Lerner Publications Company
A division of Lerner Publishing Group, Inc.
241 First Avenue North
Minneapolis, MN 55401 USA

For reading levels and more information, look up this title at www.lernerbooks.com.

Library of Congress Cataloging-in-Publication Data

Names: Fishman, Jon M., author
Title: Dak Prescott / Jon M. Fishman.
Description: Minneapolis : Lerner Publications, [2019] | Series: Sports All-Stars |
    Includes bibliographical references and index. | Audience: Ages: 7–11. | Audience:
    Grades: 4 to 6.
Identifiers: LCCN 2017051929 (print) | LCCN 2017054033 (ebook) |
    ISBN 9781541524620 (eb pdf) | ISBN 9781541524545 (library binding : alk.
    paper) | ISBN 9781541528000 (paperback : alk. paper)
Subjects: LCSH: Prescott, Dak—Juvenile literature. | Football players—United
    States—Biography—Juvenile literature. | Quarterbacks (Football)—United
    States—Biography—Juvenile literature.
Classification: LCC GV939.P74 (print) | LCC GV939.P74 F57 2019 (ebook) | DDC
    796.332092 [B]—dc23

LC record available at https://lccn.loc.gov/2017051929

Manufactured in the United States of America
1-44530-34780-4/25/2018

CONTENTS

COWBOY
COMEBACK

Prescott (left) fought hard to turn around the playoff game against the Green Bay Packers.

Dallas Cowboys fans at AT&T Stadium were quiet. The home team was losing 21–3 to the Green Bay Packers in the 2017 **playoffs**. But Dallas quarterback Dak Prescott would give the fans something to cheer about.

In the second quarter, Prescott showed the Packers his strong arm. First, he launched a 21-yard pass to teammate Dez Bryant. Then he connected with Bryant again for a 40-yard touchdown pass.

Prescott was a **rookie**. Most young quarterbacks need time to adjust to the National Football League (NFL). Yet Prescott had

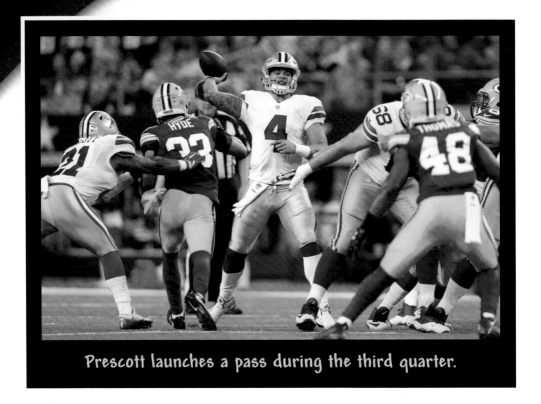

Prescott launches a pass during the third quarter.

shown all season that he wasn't like most young quarterbacks. He was ready to be a star.

The Cowboys scored again in the third quarter. With the score Green Bay 28, Dallas 13, Prescott drove his team down the field. He hit Jason Witten with a touchdown pass to make it 28–20. Dallas fans hooted and cheered.

Prescott did it once more in the fourth quarter. He led the Cowboys on an 80-yard drive. His third touchdown pass of the game made the score 28–26. Then he blasted his way past Green Bay to score the **two-point**

conversion and tie the game!

The teams traded **field goals**. Then Green Bay kicked another field goal in the final seconds. They won the game, 34–31.

It had been a great first season in the NFL for Prescott. The loss to Green Bay was hard to take. But coming from behind to almost win the game had proven something to Prescott. "We're not going to stop no matter what the score is, no matter the game," he said. "It shows the true character of this team."

Prescott learned a lot in his first NFL season.

The Dallas Cowboys have been to the Super Bowl eight times. Only the New England Patriots have gone to the big game more often. The Cowboys' five Super Bowl wins are tied for the second most in NFL history, with the Pittsburgh Steelers ahead of them in wins.

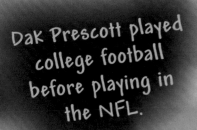

Dak Prescott played college football before playing in the NFL.

Rayne Dakota (Dak) Prescott was born in southwestern Louisiana in 1993. He grew up in Haughton, Louisiana, with his mother and two older brothers. Dak's father lived nearby and was a big part of Dak's life.

The Prescotts lived in Pine Creek Mobile Home Estates. The area had many small homes similar to where Dak and his family lived. He played football with his brothers, Jace and Tad, in a field behind their home.

Neighbor Mary Wright watched the boys play. "I just remember Dakota out there throwing the football, and Jace was so much bigger and taller than him, but [Dakota] tried to take him down anyway," Wright said.

Tad and Jace starred for the Haughton High School **varsity** football team. The varsity coaches knew about Dak when he was still in seventh grade. They

Dak became the starting quarterback for his high school football team as a sophomore after the senior starting quarterback became injured.

couldn't wait until he was old enough to play for the high school team. Dak was strong and athletic. He also had the heart of a champion. "He wanted to be the best at everything he did," Haughton High School football coach Rodney Guin said. "It didn't matter if he was playing basketball or tug-of-war; he wanted to win."

In 2008, Dak stepped in as the varsity team's quarterback. As a sophomore, he was younger than many of his teammates. Yet he quickly became a team leader. By his senior season, Dak had helped turn Haughton into one of the best teams in the state. They didn't lose a game in the regular season. He threw an incredible 39 touchdowns.

Dak is named after Dakota Dude, a cartoon bull on the show Wild West C.O.W.-Boys of Moo Mesa. Dak and Dakota have at least one thing in common: strength. "The strongest bull was Dakota," Tad said.

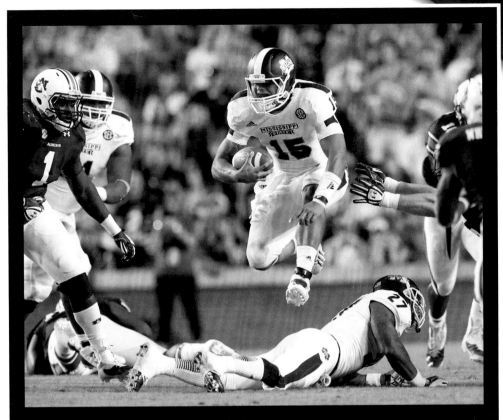

Dak had an impressive college career at Mississippi State.

Dak's amazing performances drew the attention of college **scouts**. Mississippi State was one of the first schools to show interest in him. Later, Louisiana State University (LSU) **recruited** Dak. LSU is one of college football's most successful teams. But Dak chose the Mississippi State Bulldogs. He wanted to help build a successful team rather than join a team that was already on top.

Prescott played well for Mississippi State for four seasons. But Mississippi State wasn't a school that usually produced professional players. So in 2016 when he entered the **NFL Draft**, he waited as teams chose player after player. Seven quarterbacks were picked. But still, Prescott waited. Finally, the Dallas Cowboys chose him with the 135th overall pick. Being passed over by so many teams made Prescott angry. He was ready to prove that a Mississippi State quarterback could succeed in the NFL. He was ready to work.

Scouts knew that Prescott had a strong throwing arm, but many teams still passed him over during the draft.

The ESPN Wide World of Sports Complex works with athletes of all ages and skill levels.

To make sure he was ready for his first NFL season in 2016, Prescott went to Disney World! He took part in a football camp at the ESPN Wide World of Sports Complex at Walt Disney World Resort. He worked to improve as a quarterback at the camp.

Prescott does a variety of exercises to target different parts of his body. Running and bike riding are good **cardio** workouts. They help Prescott play late into games without wearing down. Lifting weights strengthens the muscles he needs to throw deep down the field.

Prescott also works to strengthen his core muscles. Core muscles are in the back and stomach. They help athletes keep their balance and avoid injuries. Players use equipment such as heavy sleds and **medicine balls** to make their core muscles strong.

In addition to working on his strength, Prescott practices throwing so that he's ready come game time.

Prescott works on footwork drills to be quick on his feet.

Prescott led the Cowboys to a 13-3 season in 2016.

Working out at the Wide World of Sports Complex paid off. Cowboys quarterback Tony Romo was injured during a 2016 **preseason game**. Prescott took over and quickly made fans wonder how he had fallen to the 135th pick in the NFL Draft. He led Dallas to a 13–3 record and the playoffs.

Prescott's first pro season was a huge success. Instead of relaxing and celebrating, he got right back to work. NFL teams hold workouts and practices in the **off-season**. That still leaves players with plenty of free time. Prescott fills that time with more workouts. He practices the throws and steps he uses on the field.

The Cowboys put their players through a series of tests before the start of each season. The tests measure things such as a player's strength, speed, and quickness. In 2017, Prescott improved in all of these areas. His off-season workouts had paid off, and he was ready to show it on the field.

Prescott often chows down on spaghetti before games. He likes it with ranch dressing and chicken. He says that soup is one of his favorite foods. He eats soup about five times a week.

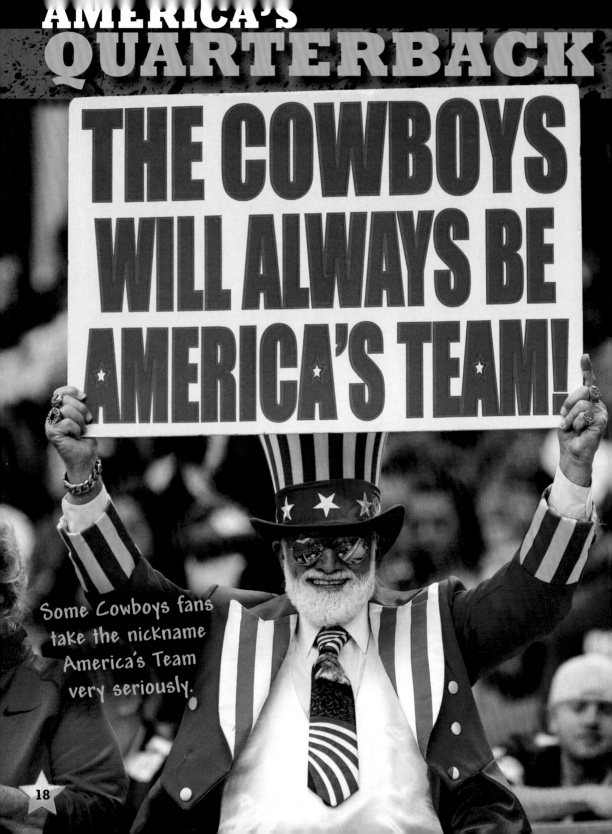

AMERICA'S QUARTERBACK

Some Cowboys fans take the nickname America's Team very seriously.

Fans cheer on the Cowboys at AT&T Stadium.

Fans call the Dallas Cowboys America's Team. The team's history of success and star players make them popular. The Cowboys are also incredibly valuable. They're worth about $4.2 billion. That means Dallas is the most valuable sports team in the world.

Prescott was excited to accept his ESPY award for the 2017 Best Breakthrough Athlete.

Prescott's popularity has soared as the quarterback of America's Team. In 2017, he won the ESPY award for Best Breakthrough Athlete. The award is given each year to an athlete who suddenly becomes a superstar.

Prescott's status as a sports hero has given him the chance to **endorse** many products. Maybe you've seen him in commercials for Pepsi or Tostitos. He also helps sell one of his favorite foods, Campbell's Chunky Soup. He works with New Era Cap, DirecTV, and many other companies. In fact, Prescott endorses so many products that he makes more money working with companies than he does playing football.

He uses his money and fame to give back to his community. "Ready. Raise. Rise." is a campaign to fight cancer. Prescott and other stars joined the drug company Bristol-Myers Squibb to take part in events to support people with cancer and find cures for the disease. The cause is close to Prescott's heart. His mother died of cancer in 2013.

Prescott has made himself even more famous through his work with products such as Pepsi.

Prescott earned two college degrees at Mississippi State. He studied leadership and **psychology.** The subjects have helped him succeed on and off the field. But he says he isn't done studying. Prescott wants to return to school to become a doctor of psychology.

Growing up, Prescott and his family didn't have much money. The experience taught him not to take anything for granted. He works hard to star in the **NFL.** But no matter what happens with football, Prescott's education will help him succeed.

Prescott likes to return to Mississippi State as much as he can.

Prescott is a big soccer fan.
His favorite team is FC Dallas.

Prescott looks for other ways to help people too. He pitches in at events to support young students. He shows up at free football camps to help athletes learn to be leaders. Prescott is committed to making the world a better place.

The leader of America's Team also gets many chances to have fun. He appears on TV talk shows such as *Good Morning America*. He goes back to Mississippi State to cheer for the school's sports teams. He's also a big supporter of FC Dallas of Major League Soccer.

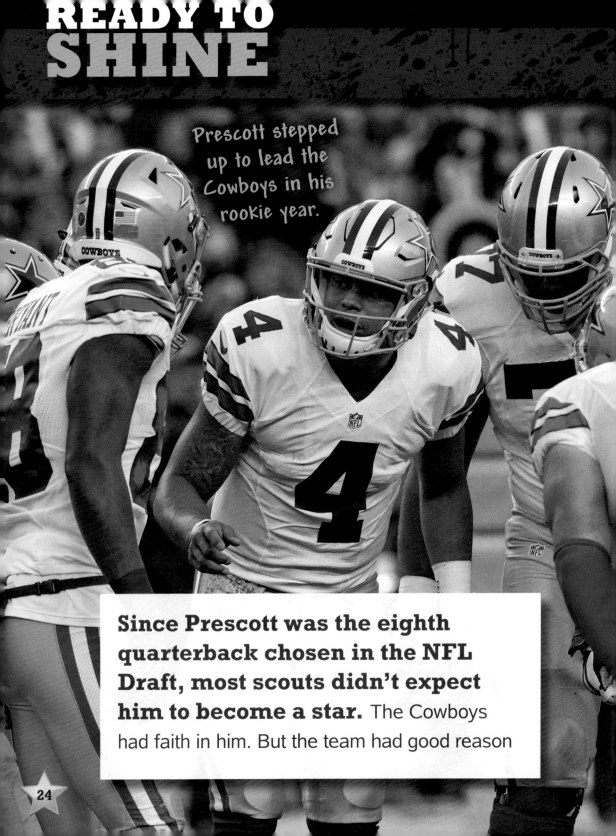

Prescott stepped up to lead the Cowboys in his rookie year.

Since Prescott was the eighth quarterback chosen in the NFL Draft, most scouts didn't expect him to become a star. The Cowboys had faith in him. But the team had good reason

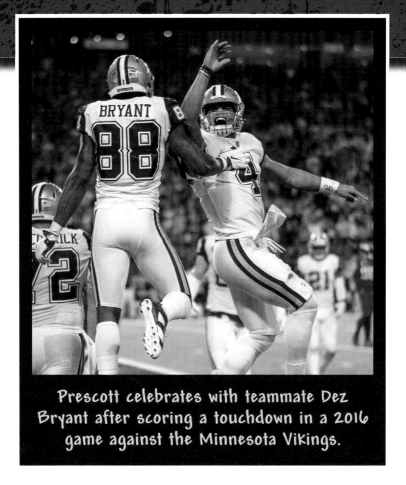

Prescott celebrates with teammate Dez Bryant after scoring a touchdown in a 2016 game against the Minnesota Vikings.

to worry when Tony Romo went down with an injury before the 2016 season. Rookie NFL quarterbacks aren't usually ready to lead their teams.

But Prescott wasn't an average rookie. He threw 23 touchdowns his first year. He was also careful with his passes, throwing just four **interceptions**. He was so good that he held onto the job even after Romo had healed from his injury. Romo later retired from football.

Prescott helped Dallas to the second-best record in 2016. Then he almost led the team to victory against the Packers in the playoffs. He won the Offensive Rookie of the Year award. He also made it to the Pro Bowl as one of the league's best players. He set several rookie records.

In 2016, Prescott became the first quarterback in NFL history to throw fewer than five interceptions in his first five hundred passing attempts.

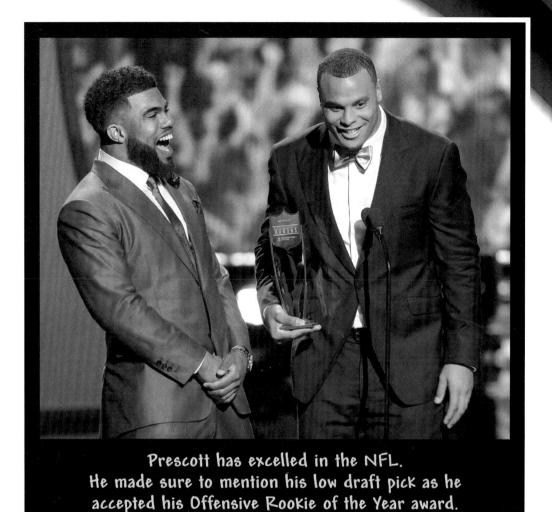

Prescott has excelled in the NFL.
He made sure to mention his low draft pick as he
accepted his Offensive Rookie of the Year award.

Some people still don't have faith in Prescott. They say his rookie season was so good that he won't be able to repeat it. And several injuries on the Cowboys team hurt his performance in the 2017 season. But the leader of America's Team isn't worried. He knows what it takes to be a superstar. "All I've ever known is hard work," Prescott said, "and hard work pays off."

All-Star Stats

The NFL has the best football players in the world. Everything happens much faster in pro football than it does in college. So rookie quarterbacks usually take time to adjust to the NFL. Prescott was ready to go on day one. Here's how his passing touchdowns compared to other first-year quarterbacks in 2016.

Touchdown Passes by Rookie Quarterbacks in 2016

Player	Team	Touchdowns
Dak Prescott	Dallas Cowboys	23
Carson Wentz	Philadelphia Eagles	16
Cody Kessler	Cleveland Browns	6
Jared Goff	Los Angeles Rams	5
Paxton Lynch	Denver Broncos	2
Trevone Boykin	Seattle Seahawks	1
Connor Cook	Oakland Raiders	1

Three players with no touchdown passes

Source Notes

7   Associated Press, "Clutch Rodgers Leads Packers Past Cowboys," *ESPN*, January 16, 2017, http://www.espn.com/nfl/recap?gameId=400927749.

9   Drew Davison, "Why Dak Prescott's Got This for Cowboys: Mom, Family, Community," *Fort Worth Star-Telegram*, last modified October 8, 2017, http://www.star-telegram.com/sports/nfl/dallas-cowboys/article101102607.html.

10   William Browning, "Dak Prescott's Hometown Beginnings," *Columbus (MS) Dispatch,* October 8, 2014, http://www.cdispatch.com/news/article.asp?aid=37035.

10   Browning.

27   Associated Press, "Set for Encore, Cowboys' Prescott Ignores 'Sophomore Slump,'" *USA Today*, September 7, 2017, https://www.usatoday.com/story/sports/nfl/2017/09/07/set-for-encore-cowboys-prescott-ignores-sophomore-slump/105372904.

Glossary

cardio: a workout designed to strengthen the heart and lungs

endorse: support and help sell a company's products

field goals: kicks that go between the goalposts at either end of the field. A field goal is worth three points.

interceptions: passes caught by the other team

medicine balls: heavy balls used to strengthen muscles

NFL Draft: an event in which NFL teams take turns choosing new players

off-season: the part of the year when a sports league is not playing

playoffs: a series of games to decide a champion

preseason game: a practice game that takes place before the regular season

psychology: the study of the human mind

recruited: tried to add a player to a team

rookie: a first-year player

scouts: people who judge the talent of athletes

two-point conversion: a play after a touchdown that is worth two points if successful

varsity: the top team at a school

Further Information

Braun, Eric. *Super Football Infographics*. Minneapolis: Lerner Publications, 2015.

Dallas Cowboys
http://www.dallascowboys.com

Fishman, Jon M. *Dez Bryant*. Minneapolis: Lerner Publications, 2016.

Football: National Football League
http://www.ducksters.com/sports/national_football_league.php

Mattern, Joanne. *Dak Prescott*. Hallandale, FL: Mitchell Lane, 2018.

NFL RUSH
http://www.nflrush.com

Index

Photo Acknowledgments

Image credits: iStock.com/63151 (gold and silver stars); Jim McIsaac/Getty Images, p. 2; Ezra Shaw/Getty Images, pp. 4–5; Tom Pennington/Getty Images, pp. 6, 16, 26; Ronald Martinez/Getty Images, pp. 7, 19; Bob Levey/Getty Images, pp. 8, 27; Seth Poppel Yearbook Library, p. 9; Kevin C. Cox/Getty Images, p. 11; Joe Robbins/Getty Images, p. 12; Greg Goebel/Wikimedia Commons (CC BY-SA 2.0), p. 13; Andrew Dieb/Icon Sportswire/Getty Images, pp. 14, 23; George Walker/Icon Sportswire/Getty Images, p. 15; Matthew Pearce/Icon Sportswire/Getty Images, p. 18; Kevin Winter/ Getty Images, p. 20; Frazer Harrison/Getty Images, p. 21; Richard W. Rodriguez/ Fort Worth Star-Telegram/TNS/Getty Images, p. 22; George Gojkovich/Getty Images, p. 24; Robin Alam/Icon Sportswire/Getty Images, p. 25.

Cover: Jim McIsaac/Getty Images; iStock.com/neyro2008.